SNAPSHOTS

SNAPSHOTS

Poetry by Cardigan Jack

Illustrations by Brent Bailor

AuthorHouse™
1663 Liberty Drive, Suite 200
Bloomington, IN 47403
www.authorhouse.com
Phone: 1-800-839-8640

AuthorHouse™ UK Ltd.
500 Avebury Boulevard
Central Milton Keynes, MK9 2BE
www.authorhouse.co.uk
Phone: 08001974150

First published by AuthorHouse 08/23/006

ISBN: 4-2596-020-0 (softcover)

Printed in the United States of America
Bloomington, Indiana

This book is printed on acid-free paper.

Illustrations by Brent Bailor
Cover and Interior Design by Legwork Team

FOR MY CHILDREN

Daralewa Afua, Funmilayo Abena,
and Aman-Re Kwasi Mensah

CONTENTS

ACKNOWLEDGEMENTS

Because my writing has been a private hobby, publication has never consumed me. I have heard prompting and wishes from all of my children to see a project such as this. But I eventually acquiesced to Funmilayo's voice: "Daddy, you should publish your work." For getting it started and introducing me to Matthew McDonald, who designed the book, I am most grateful.

Although I claim to be able to deliver pictures with words, I have never been able to use a pencil or paint to reproduce either what I think or see. This is part of why I hold such fascinated admiration for the illustrator in this project, Brent Bailor. Brent and I discussed the focus of certain poems and that was enough for him to create drawings that complement the text. I am honored. Thanks also to Ozra Bailor for support. She is among a group of readers whom I embrace as contributors.

Thanks, Siafa.

INTRODUCTION

This collection of poetry samples work done over a
period of over thirty years. Content dates some of it
throughout that period but most of it stands unrelated
to linear time. It has been arranged in five chapters to
group thematically similar poems, making reading easier.

Each poem employs a series of images creating mental
and eventually visual, if imaginary, pictures of beauty,
horror, and everyday life from various angles of view,
laid out to present to the reader.

There is a strong political current in most of these
because of the quality of the reflection of my perception,
appreciation, and interpretation of the movement of
history and human interaction in my imagination.
Often I write to satisfy myself that I have captured
some thought, fancy, or fantasy, as in a photograph.
Poetry is being actively used here to inform, agitate,
and inspire, as well as to entertain and amuse.

The more romantic reader will find appeal in the
"Blues Spectrum: from Indigo to the Sky." The poems
survey the blues from their deepest longing in the indigo
blue of despair, to the fantasy of flight into yonder blue

skies. They also attempt to integrate the range of New World longing for Africa with romantic love, as in "Michelle."

Some of these poems were based on actual events, experiences, or persons. But many are also fictitious contrivances of pure artistry seeking a political or romantic tributary to the page. Often they were notes written to myself, stirred up by an event, occasion, or emotion and overflowing as in "Jazz Tears."

I invite you to enjoy what, for me, was years of intense play. Readers may find much fodder for honest discussion and teachers may want to guide students through the imagery, vocabulary, themes and techniques used to frame these pictures into useable SNAPSHOTS.

CHAPTER ONE

TO PROTECT, HONOR, AND DEFEND THE YARD

FERTILITY

They left
An epitaph
On the scene of
Your life
Where they buried
The aborted fetus
Of our glory.

It reads:
In the dollar
May have been
Your freedom.

But don't worry,
Mother Africa
Is pregnant
Again.

OSTRACISM

Against
A granite background
Our mother sits
In the ocean
Shrouded in white.

North to south,
Dividing her womb,
From the Black Sea
To the Indian Ocean,
A fine and delicate
Silver chain extends,
Dropping a golden noose
Into the Cape.

AFRICA IS MINE

I have sacrificed a race,
Some to prison walls,
Some to dope,
Some to fear,
Some to money and greed,
Others lost in vast nowheres.
Yet I retain my spirit.

I have given in submission to survival,
The fiber of my river.
My grain is caught up in the jaws of
Smokey factories and offices.
I was taught,
The meek shall inherit the earth: I learned,
The arrogant inherit its produce.

I have sacrificed my salt
To the bottom of the ocean,
To the shamelessly cruel whip,
The legal mob, and the crumbling pillar
On which the beast arose and stands.
But I have kept my dark glitter
And lit the earth with a crystal heart.
My hands are clean.

CONTINUED

And yet, like second nature,
My tongue is twisted to
The shape of precise
Sixty-second television commercials
That usurp my energy,
Staking out a new hat from Paris,
A school for my child,
Eventual rescue for my kind.

I have given even more than I knew I had.
Nude as I am, I scorn my clothing.
But now, I have no more to give.
I must preserve for myself
The space I occupy,
And fill the space everywhere I am,
Everywhere I go, everywhere I was.
Africa is mine.

FREEDOM FIGHTERS

Gaping souls
Of half-risen stars
Yearn in the dry seabed.

Candles burn
Reluctantly
Like wet charcoal
Though they never go out.

In a trench
Behind sandbags
Cold white bones,
A wedding band
And a rusty rifle
Lay softly on the ground.

Battlefield echoes
Still hang
In the light mountain air.

And mothers still
Weep their grief
For sons
No longer babies,
No longer men,
Forever heroes,
Freedom fighters.

EXCERPTS FROM THE PARK

Wine bottles change hands
And reefer makes its circles
In joints among the onlookers.

Soda cans and cowbells
Xylophones and congas
Speaking in a loud voice

How a chunk of Black mankind
Trapped down here
And made into everything but men.
Hear the drums.

Hear the drums
Go follow Malcolm
To the grave.
See the people marching behind
To fill their lives with their labors.
Hear the drums.

Hear the drums
And in the sound
Float mellow tones

CONTINUED

7

Of pelvic whirlwinds
Blowing from an ebony antelope
Sleek and standing still,
Amazed at truth and wondering:
Will the liberation of the people
Ever come?
Hear the drums.

Hear the drums say,
Go tell my ebony antelope
On the broad plains of skin music:

Go follow Malcolm
To the grave
See the people marching behind
To fill their lives with their labors.
Hear the drums.

FROM A PAINTING
BY DUMILE DANIEL DUMILE

Suspended
By great powerful wings
And the fury
Of a battle too intense
To stop, and
In lofty clouds
That hang
Over mountain peaks
And jagged rocks
Separated by a valley, deep
Where human
And all that suffer
Await the end of the duel,
Two eagles fight.
For what?

Through their beaks
Human eyes locked in rage
See painful visions.
Their claws
Are his nose,
His muzzled mouth.

A picture of man in
Transition,
How long can two eagles fight?
As the picture hangs,
It would seem
Forever.

CHAPTER TWO

CLAIMING SIDES

BRING ME LOVE

Good morning, rainbow.
Kindly cradle my smile
In your curl of color.
Favor me with fertile moisture.
Sprinkle my mountainsides
With your mist.

Waning moonlight,
Kissed by dewdrops that
Form on petals of roses
Threatened by October frost,
Bows to a gentle encroachment
Of the eastern sun
At the edge of the horizon.

Good morning, rainbow.
Proclaim this a great day.
Kiss away my blues
And bring me love.

RESTLESS SLEEP

Wake up, *ndugu*.
We've slept too long,
We've sexed too long.
The bed is too hot, *ndugu*.
That's why I got up.

I dreamt I saw
White, tattered sails
Strung from a stout mast
And Black bodies
In estrus on the deck.

In the hold
They were sexing,
Loving, dancing,
And the ship was drifting
Only with the current
Of the tired river.

The dream faded
And the bed was hot.
That's why I woke you, brother.
Besides, it's really hard
To sleep in a hot bed.

FOR FOFIE, KWAME, DAUDI, AND ZAMYE

Harvest of fertile fields
Where we toil in play,
Your father's eyes shine with pride
Reflecting only a dream
Of rapid rifle fire in resistance
Down where they chained us
To the boat, to the dirt,
To their sweat shops
And their bus stops.

Fruit you be,
The seed of our time,
Wine of our vine
That Tarzan can't swing on.
Angaza brings you
A handful of candles.
Keep one and share the rest
With your household.

They are the torches
That will show the way
Back to where
The strangers found us
At our play.

FOR MY MOTHER

You came
In a musical caravan of
Copper chariots
Dressed in evergreen simplicity,
The sun always on your forehead;
And you, looking up
Where we pulled you down
To the smiles in your eyelids.

And is it the pillar in your spirit
That kept the dove of Babylon
Forever out of your hands?
Is it your Nilotic shadow
That gave purpose to this penance,
Gave color to this transparent maze
Where walls grow up among the pillars
That burst from your breasts?

Owls with blazing night eyes call
From the silence of midnight,
Welcoming the virgin day,
Begging the vulture in its quest

CONTINUED

To rule the sky, to let live,
Let live the creeping creatures
Crawling around your caravan
Like a nomadic shoal of sharks
In unrelenting persistence
Behind a limping slave ship.

At dawn, the sunrise
Shall assume your facial features
With honey on your lips.
And at noon I will say a prayer
So the sun may later set in peace.

MICHELLE

Angry gray waves of ocean crossing,
Rich with shoals of sharks
That sought gifts of our dead and live alike,
Lifted us through centuries
To a place of options and choices,
All or any, yours like at a fruit tree.

Seeds of tillers of the soil
Though trampled by shepherds' beneficiary sheep
Grow up protected, delicate and fertile
Like every mother's child.

Mother's gift of fine ebony velvet,
Soft and shine, the way chocolate wants to be,
Look up and see her face.
Seek the sun and point a finger at it daily.
Get closer, see the light.

Feel the warmth of the closeness
Of my mother's breast and the breath of
Her nostrils above your head.
Look up and see her face.
Here is where love resides.

CHAPTER THREE

BLUES SPECTRUM: INDIGO TO THE SKY

DEEP PURPLE ROSE

Tropical, deep purple rose,
Silhouette imposed upon
The brilliance of sunshine;
Quiet passion follows rain
Without a smile now,
But with a crown: halo
From a rainbow
Carved from pristine sunlight.
Deep purple rose,
Won't you smile for me?

FAYCEZ

I like your face
And your smile is pretty
When you smile.

But your smile is prettiest
When you smile
For me.

RIVERBOAT

Images of your face
Like shadows of passing ships
Come and go,
Silhouettes in the sanctuary of dusk.

Heavy-laden ships force the water,
Carrying their shadows with them.
You fade in shrunken space where
Presence invokes transparency of shadows.

Bathing the dark side of ships
Where shadows fall past noon,
The water, restless in its disturbance,
Bears the familiar image of your face.

The river forms undulating shadows that inscribe
Watery expressions of your face that come and go.
And like childhood memories
I make room for yet one more.

SKY TOP ROOM

Looking up,
There is a face in the chandelier.
Under the voice
That addresses the gathering
In the loud speaker,
There is whisper.
And I hear you. How clearly I hear you.
There is a hand gently on my hand,
And safely in my hand,
A hand I keep.

Even when I go far away
I never leave.
Sunset only hides the sun;
It's always there.
The face in the chandelier
I brought with me and keep.
The whispering voice brings counsel
And I'm pleased for guidance.
I will keep the hand
I have in mine.

CONTINUED

Sunlight creeps in
Through a window in your bosom
Finding crevices
In the heart.
And light can expose much beauty;
Though at the roots to which
We cling and from which we grow
We keep no light,
But nurture subterranean privacy.

WITHOUT SLEEP TONIGHT

Quiet nights inspire reflection.
As she lies alone she hears his voice
Like a distant saxophone wail,
Drifting through a high window.
And softly she calls his name.

For long hours she couldn't sleep.
Thoughts of the stranger
Flooded her mind
And she could see his face
But she couldn't sleep.

She wondered if love was budding
Or simply playing games.
Was it longing that cheated her
Of sleep?

Love's language lingers long
In her mind.
And she seeks a label for her loneliness.
She gets up, gets dressed,
And knocks on his door,
Oasis in dry longing for his kiss.

SPRING COURTSHIP

The wind is still; silhouettes go by in color.
Twilight makes shadows of everything.
Birdcalls, treetops blanketed in mellow song,
Like body oil on your belly
Awaiting a gentle massage,
Make the aging day a thing to be shared;
Like the sidewalk fire
Where we warmed our naked hands,
The melting snowflakes dripping
Onto the blaze where we met
Before we knew each other.

It seems a whole civilization
Has gone by since then.
You are really approaching.
Your purple silhouette escapes the dusk
And enters the range of my nearsightedness.
Outstretched arms support my strong
But failing cardiac function.

I couldn't wait for you to come.
But first, let's walk a block or two.
I like to watch the flowers,
Their gloating glory glamorous
Like your gleaming smile.
And when we return
We'll kick off our shoes and relax
Over cakes and tea.
We'll talk about our new family
And invite a new member.
We're only two now, and we're alone.

REUNION

To find you here at this time,
In this place, where
I thought I was alone,
Makes us spectators to rare fate.

It has been a time when
I have known thought itself
To be a loyal companion
With whom I'd hold hands
And pour the molten liquid
Of my heart over
The solitary sanctuary
Of inner horizons
And endless peace.

And then,
The way water finds
Lowest ground,
So much comes to rest
So gently at your feet,
Much as if time stood still.
Because here you are,
Bordering on mystery at this time,
In this place;
And a celebration has begun.

CONTINUED

At first I thought,
"Just one of my fantasies,
A familiar muse I'd welcome."
But then, the genuine focus of sight
And you are before me,
At this time;
And in this place.

More unexpected than surprising and
More surprising than frightening,
And everywhere a little of each,
As shock clings, finds a place to rest.
Never thinking I'd find you here,
Like hale in the midst of summer.
Yet it's you I see, I know it. Welcome.

GIFT

I wanted to
Give you
Something simple.
But I didn't know
What was appropriate
For you.

All I had was
A necklace of seashells
And a string of pearls.

But I wanted
To give you
Something simple.
So I gave
You
Me.

SOUTHBURY

If I should dance with angels
And invite sea creatures
To surf the clouds with me,
My shadow will still fall, a tall silhouette
Where your voice lights the trail
To sweet and complete silence.

And even after the silence,
Recurring echoes of your song
Make staccato mantra reminders
Like the melody of our rapture
When we sing ourselves to sleep.

The sound of your voice
Jolts my head around
And though I hate to see you leave,
I love to watch you walk away.
I now know I could also see a song.

Secure with love we stride above the clouds
Where our shadows, cast by the same light of love
Fall singularly like the sound of our orchestra.
And in the end, we take our instruments
And go our separate ways.

We will return to the romance of our music.
Your voice will bring me back to the bandstand
Where you sing my name like a mantra
And again I play the melody of your rapture
As if written in a new key signature.

MOONGAZE

All those who would attend our romance,
Those who would share the glare of moonlight with us,
Even those who wonder of your pampered spirit
And your tantalized lips, have them come out and watch.
Invite them to see what our love looks like
When starlight finds our eyes.

Tell them to come witness what the sky is like
When clouds are gone and stars fill the space above us.
They will know as we know, that the moonlight
Passed them by and gathered its glow
For our private benefit as if
The street noise fell silent to watch them watch us.

As they watch we will play our song, plucking stars
Singularly and in harmony, orchestrating like harp strings.
Night of verses that usher instructions: listen,
This is how we love, how they might love
If they found the place of the sun's asylum that brought us
Moonlit waters, where fish don't care
if your kiss never ended.

CONTINUED

31

I am jealous of myself when I love you
and my body is never dry.
Oceans of our sweat have their own native fish
And the moonlight excludes onlookers as
piercing glow of starlight
Finds our eyes reflecting in each other,
commanding the call,
Me to you, and you to me, reciprocal.
Though they watch they never see the love
That happens without effort
In spite of our eventual exhaustion.

Not seeing, they will talk about our love.
They may deny our love, say it's not so.
Stop them, they will say, anathema after
the rest of the seventh day.
And across the crowded nighttime street,
amid the noise and chatter,
We will find each other and they will never know
when we left
To find the moonlight and gaze at stars
that stare at our twinnings.

WAITING FOR YOU

The forsythia came out
When you left.
But everywhere
Daffodils stayed around
To shadow low crocuses.
And I wondered if
You'd see them
This time.

I stayed and watched them,
And as tulip buds grew fuller,
So did my heart.
And much like the birds,
Soon you were back.

I WILL MISS YOU

The children will put beads
In your hair
And decorate your locks.

The gods will brush your lips
With wine and make you
Skirts of woven vine.

The birds will sing greetings
To the morning
And light the sun each day.

Your gentle heartbeat will bathe
In fluid rhythms
In your boiling chest.

And I?
I will miss you.

AROUSAL

Squeeze me
Early in the morning.
I love to feel African blood
Rush to my head
And watch my brown face
Turn to black.
That's when I know
I can attack
A new day
With confidence.

NIGHT SHIFT

Watching the dance of evening shadows
Morning seems remote
On either side of sunset
And I'm impatient for the night.

The painted sky blinks.
Day drops its weary veil of dusk
To block the blazing brilliance beyond.
And I cannot see tomorrow.

And so, impatient for the night,
I welcome the last hour of sunlight
Through the window curtains,
Knowing that the darker it gets
The sooner you would be home.

MOUNTAIN TOP

Flight
Of a moon-scarred cloud
Across now crisp
Untended sky
Leaves thin wind
And streaking birdsong
To fashion
Open shelter
For eager lovers.

Sunrise
Follows the moonlight
And where nocturnal romance
Once burned
To liquid residue,
Open stares now
Prompt infinite wonder.

SEASONS OF LOVE

In those eternal spring times
That blew blossoms' pollen in our hair,
Kisses seemed to punctuate sentiments,
Each with its own halo.

Behind our awnings
Everything we did was correct,
Even when we laughed at each other's anxiety
And sought refuge, pressing chests together,
Seeking to unify two runaway heartbeats.

And then, in that summer
That burned as if at both ends,
We mopped the liquid of our exhaustion
And ignored the heartbeats
We couldn't unify.

CONTINUED

Looking back, we couldn't see
The miles we had walked.
Yet we had come so far,
And to the end.
And we thanked each other
For the journey.

The summer was over eventually.
Leaves fell, and we could tell
The cold this winter
Would never turn to spring.
And although our eyes still speak
And our hearts throb nervously,
Sentiments run on with no kisses
To punctuate the cold shiver
Of our wintry lips.

SURREAL

It was in the realm of dream,
Becoming real only after
The awakening.
I savored it in slumber,
Never wanting to wake up.

Like a dream,
The orange flame of you
Evaporated like smoke
On a musty summer afternoon.

And on a morning
When the sun never shined,
I woke up to find
My dream was over
And you were gone.

Now, as I remember slumber
I simply want to
Induce another dream.
And this time,
Please don't wake me.

CHAPTER FOUR

COMMENCEMENT

The clouds are there in watchful stillness.
Although hearts of graduates thump like a stampede
All that's loud is the chatter of the waiting crowd
And the clanking of construction metal.
York College is building the Academic Core.

Academia, meanwhile, colonizes the street:
Flashes of color disturb the black of robes
Like the settling smoke of this morning's bombs
Eroding a Falkland Island shoreline; a Lebanese city
Crying like French horns as the band
Calls the carnival to motion.

In the faces and smeared about the gathering
We feel that something is not there.
Maybe it's the steel band I miss. There is no rhythm.
Roaming thought of years left behind
frighten the moment
As it trembles under smiles above robes
More like the procession behind the deceased
Whom we all knew.

CONTINUED

But there's the Star-Spangled Banner,
No wind to move it today.
Stench stagnant, though not for long.
Politicians sit before us, we before them.
Not as tired as patient,
More hopeful than jaded,
And both.

The sun peeps timidly.
Bald heads covered in ceremonial caps don't burn
But sweat, imprisoned over gowns that flash
Images of call girls receiving
The sacrament of Holy Communion.

As she rises, dignitaries in the valedictorian's shadow,
Behind flowers, microphones, certificates with red bows
Matching the façade around the dais perk up.
She speaks: Maya Angelou and Chinese proverbs
Among the quotations.
She calls for change from those who like it like it is.
And though we've had enough
We wait, sitting proudly.

CONTINUED

Then the president talks of South Africa
and the nuclear outlook.
I remember the Middle Passage!
Lofty talk from the guest speaker,
glib tongue borrowed from
The New World African church besieging
the subhuman spirit
To let live, let live human dignity.
All spill from loud speakers everywhere,
and into the heavy air which,
If it trapped the dominant message
We'd never leave our seats. And
Like the deprecation at a comedy gala
We clap burning hands in response.

Near incongruous, the applause frightens me.
I wonder and restrain my pen. I'll just listen
And celebrate a graduating class.

JIMMY'S PLACE

The wind is restless.
The extent of the block,
Cars huddle in driveways, under trees,
Nestle in shade near houses;
The narrow street seems just in case.

Sparrows chirp and flitter
In a blooming Rose of Sharon bush
Across the street, yet nearby.
An occasional dash of flaming red
Sends a cardinal in flight.
The blue jay won't stay long either.

The robin runs in the grass and stops
To lift his head in exhibition of a brilliant breast
That can't deflect eyes that seek the breast,
While others less familiar, do their business,
Often a mocking chant, mantra in approval
Of the absence of response.
Among them, one alone would dare
To dodge between the web
Of electric and telephone cables
Only to sing his song on an exclusive sound stage.

CONTINUED

Cars go by like a railroad, impersonal, distant.
Their most persistent sound blends into the stillness.
But even after birdsong is isolated from engines,
The high hiss of crickets in chorus
Still remain ever present as the sky.

Mountains of silvery clouds
Shelter the undulating neighborhood tree line.
Their various greens bulge, point, and spread
As they dance summer's sun song
Measured by the wind.

On the housetops,
Short chimneys keep watch
Around shiny wind-spun attic fans.
And above it all, the town's incinerator chimney,
Imposing as the law, ignores the wind
And just looks around the neighborhood
Seeing nothing.

THOUGHTS

When night pours down
Dense and heavy and dark,
Its quietude suggests
A question for the morning.
And so, we sleep.

We sleep quiet and heavy
Through the dark of night
Hardly waiting for daylight.
Then morning comes, inevitably,
With well-considered answers.

Mornings always ponder night's questions.
Daylight is clear in spite of clouds.
Where darkness was, now light appears.
All is clear and another question forms,
Blinding as the night.

Wait through night's sleep:
Dream until morning.
After every nocturnal question
Day rises with the answer.

Is it the night or
Is it the morning that thinks?

VISORS

When at first
A driver learns to drive
He looks at the car
He is driving
While he is driving.

When a driver has
Learned to drive
He looks at the big picture
Ahead in the road.
The immediate is past.

We look out to horizons so far.
And the next moment
Always seems so far away,
Because there is so much
To see before we see
So far away.

BROOKLYN BRIDGE

The bridge has
Two arches,
One that comes
And one that goes
Either of two places.

There is no detour
And no turning back.
No one gets lost
Until leaving
The bridge.

JAZZ TEARS

It is not always that
I want to cry. It is when
My constant weeping heart
Overflows banks of sandbagged eyelids
In floods of pain
The dams of my soul
Can't contain.

But it is easy to make me cry.
Daydreaming, I see Langston Hughes
Hauling a wagon
Laden with the talent of our years
And nameless faces basking
In inexhaustible and historic admiration
As if Bessie smith or Ella proclaimed,
"Justice, my children."
And a stream appears on my cheek.

CHERYL BYRON

Stars appear, moonrise, sunrise,
Measures left behind bill collectors.
I missed the performance at the museum,
Urban prisoner in a car
And no place to park it.

But finally I have the performer,
Silent staging, Middle Passage link.
Down from gold streaks in her hat,
Gold-strung locks cover earrings that
Curl above a brazen neck plate.

The room, like a lighted cave,
Stands facing windows of others,
Mostly deserted in restful pale of evening.
She removes the hat.
The windows stand, unmoving.

Her locks hang over velvet colors:
Purple, ivory, silver, the assortment of
New World stones on her fingers.
I have the show, private off-stage gathering.

Stories the ancients told
Cascade gently,
They picture us and her,
We bear the baggage.

GROWING UP

Boyhood flies like spring birds.
Mother's voice, a breeze
On which I spread my wings.
Wind passes; trees settle.
I fly to a treetop and sing.

Hot summer winds rustle grass.
Close to the bosom of the ground
I huddle with my brothers
Scratching earth for morsels,
Barely disturbing grass roots.

Autumn passes; heat abates.
Boyhood fades; winds grow cold.
The memory of my mother's voice
Speaks to my children as they huddle.
And we fortify provisions
For the winter to come.

ROBERT'S DOTTY

I had missed the green mat
In Robert's fourth-floor hallway.
Thought she'd pulled it in the door
Like everybody else seemed to do.

They fought real bitter and she
Always visited to compete with the TV
For attention and affection,
Though he snapped disgust
And often put her out.

And she would say he couldn't do it
While he would say he didn't want it.
And then she was alone in his bed,
Her bangles tangled with rings and chains.

Her presence lingered lazy:
Slender shoes and cigarettes
Foreign looking,
Like pages of the truce
Scattered among bodies and weapons
That killed them where they died.

CONTINUED

Absence of the artifacts,
Routine as the spaces
Between our contact,
Didn't raise a second eyebrow
Until he took it upon himself
To tell me
Why she'd stayed with him.

She had gambled past her limit,
Sank into a hole,
Deep, with no money in it.
Too proud to face the judge,
She let the landlord win.
She hurt, wept, and moved in with her sister
When the streets spread
Wide like throughways.

AN ORDER FOR THE PAINTER

Paint me a picture of me
Though I'll never be the same again.
Use the oils of my boyhood
And since I always look up,
Make it a mural on the sky.

Paint the crimson African sun
Blazing down on freedom fighters
And homeless, hungry families
Facing the deserts of our rejection
Like lost pages of an old address book.

Paint the wasted men
Staring from prison walls,
Looking out of windows
Where nothing moves
Because beyond the bars is concrete.

Paint against a background of women
With Black babies in their bodies,
Trucking over stained slush and mire
That fell white over three hundred years ago.

CONTINUED

And in the streets there are blind eyes
Following the circles of the sisters' hips
Trying to sniff the smell they missed
At birth.

And don't you forget the contract
Written on the ice:
Broken promises evaporating
Like the summer snows of forever
Reminding me in slow degrees,
That I'll never be the same again.

Paint me a picture of me
In the deep hollows
Behind a million suns
Setting on a Caribbean horizon.
Paint me picture.

CHAPTER FIVE

ENDPAPER

EARLINE

I think of you in springtime
When winter's spell of dormant sleep
Wakes up to new decorations.
Crocuses poking through the snow
Only signal phantasmagoria of
Adornment yet to come.

Here come the daffodils, hyacinth fragrance
To color beds of tulips and their avalanche
Of mostly blue and white bells with the yellow
In between. And when the mountain laurel
Drapes its locks in bunches,
I think of you in springtime.

When around cultivated plots
The evergreens, pines, and endless assortment
Of bushes, each as distinctive as my sisters,
Your big sister locks fall about your forehead,
Surely there to grace the smile of you I keep
Complete with the mountain laurel
Draped about your forehead.

CONTINUED

I walk and sing to my soul, wishing I had my guitar.
I make myself the promise to reclaim
The state of freedom I had found
In the vigor of an early April afternoon traipse
Through the familiar neighborhood.

I think of you each time when on the parkways
I begin to lose the view of houses in
other neighborhoods
As leaves grow out and the curtain of trees
Begins to flaunt its pantheon of color,
Shades of green, adorned with mountains of blossoms.
I have a wish to enjoy this with you.

Somehow, it seems to resemble another picture,
A picture of the house in Jackass Alley.
Or yet another picture of Grandma's
Tiers of shelves with plants
From Jesseme and the roses to anthuriums
And the midnight Cinderella;
Pictures we may both remember.

CONTINUED

And now, in spite of shared treasures
Of childhood innocence and the beauty
Of the tropical rain forest still extant,
In this new jungle I see the yellow forsythia
As a laughing background to shiny red rosehips
Glistening in the burnt orange of sunset.
It is a picture I want to share with you.
And I think of you in springtime.

At dawn, the night bird's monotony of song
Plays its cacophony over the din din, ting ting ting
Of backyard wind chimes,
dancing to a mint gale left over
From the savage departure of March.
Above it all, naked tree branches dance
And there is a fertility resembling gestation
As the crisp wind tosses the mountain laurel
Across your forehead and over he smile
I keep of you.
And I think of you in springtime.

SUMMER'S DAWNING

Shadows of spring fall long into June.
Dusty blooms fade.
Leaves claim winter's residue
Of dormant branches, their months of prayer
Answered by a warm southerly front.

In the fields and off the paths,
Shortcuts carve tangential tracks.
A web of bald spots blisters
The fresh new grass, leaving a document
Of shrinking time from here to there.

The heavy wool behind the closet door
Makes way for cotton veils on virgin bosoms,
While jaded ones join jealously,
After babies' abandoned milk jugs
Fix their eyes away from mine
And to the ground.

Laughter is easier; late nights more popular.
Next spring's babies find a sweaty genesis.
We cheat the day an hour into evening
Waiting longer for the dark,
As the sky's collage peeps down
Among the trees.

FALL

Fall around the park, and all round the park
Berries and late bloomers mingle color
with turning leaves.
The bouquet that rings the open playground
Keeps a seal between the outer ring of architecture
And busy roadways, and the inner core of pure play.

A silent football lofted far raises cries of young men
Reaching for it like guests at a wedding ritual,
Trying to claim a flying garter from
the bride's upper thigh.
And the children run. The children run and laugh.
They outdo each other and outdo themselves.
The park is a place of joy.

Even lovers find the open space sufficient shelter
For gazing in each other's eyes.
Early architecture graces hillsides
That slope down to where we run laps breathless,
Or proclaim nose to nose, "I love you."

Open shelter for lovers, freedom for children,
Open space for footballs, flat surfaces for runners,
And a runway for wild flowers that resemble
The pattern on the spread we'd turn back when
The sun leaves, falling behind far trees,
And we must go home to evening's repose.

DETROIT

Over there,
Where the heavy waste of the city rises,
Dim lights peep out
Rubbing sore eyelids
Against the darkness.

The blazing pyramid stands
Tall above the arena,
While Black hands scrounge in the dust
Among angels carrying baskets
To the cathedral.

Down under the smog
Where the cars are made,
Flowers come out in springtime
And wilt in characteristic innocence,
Leaving summer's leaves
To bear the torch
Till winter reigns again.

CONTINUED

Over there,
Where Black hands scrounge
For morsels for the façade,
Concrete climbs steel beams
And Black mothers shine latrines
Overlooking lawns of dandelion polka dot
That cover the excess from fat round tables.

From fourteen flights
Up on a hotel steel beam,
Detroit whimpers muted screams,
And the skyline weeps at sunset
With the coming of the night.

CATSKILL CAMPING

Purple red of fuchsia tent wall
Silhouettes the waning flame of
An August campfire
Dying in the rain.

The great roar of mountain thunder
Sounds close as static
On the radio
Where they say it's raining.
Pitter, patter, confirmation.

Raindrops in rapid succession
Now leak through the close undergrowth
And meanders in streams that flow away
To the glistening lake
With diamonds that flow away
And shine again.

CONTINUED

Long miles and many hours from home,
We savor confidence that,
Soon will come some definite ends:
The U. S. Open,
Donkey Convention in Chicago,
The Yankees, Mets,
Definite ends.

But Spice, our canine friend,
Hungry turtles and birds,
Two dozen zebra finches
All waiting.
I'm going home to see
If this rain is falling
On my garden as well.

BEAUTIFUL BRIDGE

The glare behind the sudden disappearance of the sun
    Fades where clouds get gray and dense.
Absence of the stream of light that strings the bridge,
    Attributed to a persistent but ephemeral sunbeam.

      Watch for the lighting, we'd say.
      It's marvelous when it lights up.
      Right now, the shape of the structure
      Is the marvel next to where we sit.

      And they streak across the river,
      Streams of light on support cables,
      Rising to a hump in the center
      As we face the darkness of the ocean.

      Birds float, lovers flirt, and the sun sets
      Through a burnt hole in the clouds
That lets its blaze change from a patchy streak
      To the full crimson circle we saw.

    And without even knowing it, it was gone.
Our making of the godhead of sunset's destiny
      Follows the path of the sun
      To the horizon of its inevitable rest.

REFLECTIONS OF SUMMER
WITH JACKIE

Quietly, the question stumbles
From her lips with uncertainty.
After many days of waiting for showers,
Only clouds and longing for the sun.
Together on the grass we stand and wonder,
Wet feet and mist like crystal powder
On crimson petals of geraniums.

We walk the stretch of garden beds
And flirt with color and design.
Was it her crochet needles
That painted this flower scene,
Knitting ones, or just a hand spade?
A rose that seems to blaze
Looks up among companions,
Their question, an echo from her mirror.

And so, the artist with the flowers
Drops the spade and awaits the showers.
In spite of the mist from the water hose
She raises both hands to make one sound
As if to utter a fervent prayer,
And the question stumbles out:
Will it rain today?

JACKIE'S GARDEN

It seems an endless party of gleeful smiles,
The backyard garden, dancing in the breeze.
Beside the laughing dahlia,
Petals of her earlier sister
Adorn the leaves and spray the ground
The way a bridal gown leaves the altar.

Here, the roses are tiny. They laugh,
Bunched into numerous bouquets,
No less shy than girlish adolescence,
The giggly pink with yellow marigolds
Lined up at its feet; and rocks
Defining the garden space
Like shoes of the honor guard.

Not yet in full bloom, buds
Cradled in foliage, their windblown rhythms
Intense as the eyes of graduates
Going to the prom, they sway.
Not as seasoned as the open rose, they blush;
Eagerness for the spectacle of nudity, reserved.

Early summer, fine weather,
Trees, like lovers playing in the open air,
Flowers at the margins, and children in the sand.
Clouds are elsewhere, birdsong everywhere,
And the garden whispers softly
At the earlobes of the hedge.

EXILE

Years can't tell the time
I've been away.
This skeletal frame of mine
Can't tell how long it's been.
Breathless Carib land,
Place of my exile,
No African mornings dawn
Under clouds that cover
The red man's land,
And I know I'm not at home.

In the silence before daybreak
I sit and listen for the rumbling
Of the Nile.
But the Thames keeps rushing
Past my window with
A heavy, sinking crown
Rolling along with bald stones.

CONTINUED

I lick my lips for Zambezi waters
And in my tongue I find
The busy Mississippi
Flowing from my mouth.
And I am afraid of my voice.

Through hollow tree trunks
Capped with hides
I hear my children cry:
We'll walk the way, they say,
On the wounds that built this tomb.

I hear their voices
Calling from inside the hills,
Gaining, reaching, louder and stronger.
There's unison in their voices.
They call for Africa
And I know I'm not at home.

OH, DIANA!

No where but here this morning,
Scrappy Albuquerque Mountains,
High all round and naked,
In contrast to Tennessee's Dark Smoky
Where cotton, white in the valley,
Defines the river, long and dark.
Swift with the blood of
Fleeing Africans, the fertile ranges rise,
Themselves like shadows of dark peoples.

Forty West, New Mexico:
Native Pueblo home of another age,
Now conjure images of the dreadful nerve of
Move west movies;
Only the bare hills have no yelling Indians,
No dying savages.
The yellow dirt seems to remember the slaughter,
And unforgiving, the sporadic pinion yield
Dots the sorry graveyards of trampled pride.
Waking, Albuquerque winks a question
At sunrise.

CONTINUED

The city rises from the mountain;
Hot and dry, the air still sweet
As if just belched up from the gulf.
Though the dirt everywhere is colored
New from the bulldozer blade,
Adobe atavisms from that other age remain.
And in and among them conquest mixes people
From far away and long ago: no strangers;
But today, I've come to visit.

GLIMMERGLASS

Clouds just having cleared,
I walk to the east,
My hands above my eyes.
Before me, the mountain sprawls,
Marking off the big sky
On one side.

The valley where I camp
Howls with the restless north wind
That drives the big sky
Once so blue,
Back to shield the sun.
And suddenly, I can stare at
Where the sun just was.

Behind me also, I can see the campfire
That was hidden in the sun.
A pile of logs ablaze for many hours
Now threatened by the mighty sky,
Ready to puke at any minute.

STORM

Usually, it happens at night.
The flying wind that taunts a windowpane,
Drifts a dream's detour through crevices
That squeal on the brawl outside.

Today I saw my new willow tree dance,
Slender and virginal on stage
Among robust maples and the weathered shrubbery,
Impatient, as a candidate for marriage.

The London plane tree curls its bark and swings
Balls of seeds through leaves that sing a song
They know only in a blown assault.
And seduced, my willow dances helplessly.

SECRETS

In view of crablike eyes that rise
To scan the mangrove swamp of conversation
Mushrooms of private worlds bulge
Like earthen nests of ants,
Peaceful only to themselves.

In curling shadows of cloisters
Heavy robes slowly trace a twisting track.
At the end of a silken waist cord,
Questionable keys beat a padded rhythm
In folds of fabric that fumbles between thighs
With every measured stride.

People stop to look, continue to wonder.
Sequels meander through the days.
Illusive moments connect like Rubik's Cubes
In many stumbling tries
Though often never disclose
The raw passion that lingers in languid eyes.

MAYBE ABLE

I have fished my childhood in the pond
And never saw the fish I'd catch
Until it's fate was on my hook.
And as I mourned the few that
Slipped back into the water,
I found delight in those that laid in my basket
Waiting for thyme and onions
Fired in a gently oiled skillet.

In pineapple fields and sugar cane patches
That were not my own, I browsed,
Seeking only the finest fruit
To embellish my relaxation
In the clearing beneath
Some sprawling, shady tree.

And I've watched you come and go
Among the rest, object of easy comparison.
In my repose now I think of you
And long for earth's warm bank
Around the pond I used to fish.
On a musty evening we could lay
In rich perfume of ripe pineapples,
Any trench our cradle.

CONTINUED

Voices low, sweat flowing freely,
Roof open sky, our cover.
And to breathe without knowing it,
We could drift to blissful sleep
And wake to find the sun gone;
Happy that we never needed clean sheets,
Just each other.

EKG RESULTS

My heart works fine.
It only hurts
In the presence of
Bigotry and injustice.

THE WRITING IN THE STREETS

Through last century's most defining decade,
we came up
Kicking and screaming about everything.
We rebelled against all that was
And made it all over in our own image,
now mutant mirrors of our years.
Back then, our music gorged social mountainsides
like volcanic rivers of antiquity;
It's indelibility, morphing the essential genealogy
of future entertainment
From bee bop to Motown, and onto the Hip Hop
Nation, echoes of mutant mirrors.

And in that dark instructive decade when we marched,
from Soweto to Selma,
What was it that burned churches,
watched us hang from trees,
And killed us everywhere like midnight cockroaches
invading decent homes?
Precious status quo, honored tradition,
demanded and imposed law and order as we
Disturbed the peace and rattled the curious quietude
like umbrellas in a thunderstorm.
In the end, our voices were sacrificed behind the foam
in our mouths, hence our mutant mirrors.

CONTINUED

And even though that decade of our becoming
became heavy as our chains,
We carried it, making it look light as ashes
that blew in the wind then.
Ashes from burning draft cards and bras,
burning tenements and storefronts, burning.
And as we inhaled the fumes of our time
our giddy heads and saturated loins
gave birth and in our children we didn't know
ourselves or them. What mirrors? Now,
Reading walls, like mutant mirrors, we wander
through neighborhoods and wonder what we see.

In the streets, our sons traipse, their clothing hang from
their bodies like bastard flags.
We hear them talk with words which,
in our rebellion we never used.
They identify themselves by names we thought
were fighting words when we were young.
On exhibition likewise, our daughters paint
denim fabric on their naked backsides,
Themselves, waving bastard flags
to anonymous and disaffected audiences.
We see a new nation rise up with no sire
to claim fatherhood. Whose child is that?

CONTINUED

From our lynching and our marches,
our rebellion and civilizing rhetoric, to our silences
Was born, the Hip Hop Nation,
satellite seeking safe orbit in the new century. And
Today, tracing old worn black tracks
back to wellsprings of our own early inspiration,
We come face to face with an illusive imperative
to retrace Middle Passage pathways,
Birth canal to eternal exile, and tempered incubator
of New World salvation. So counsel
Enlightenment and prosperity, love and tolerance,
pride and dignity. And claim tomorrow, now.

PURCHASE INFORMATION PAGE

Purchase this book from your favorite bookstore, or online from AuthorHouse, Barnes & Noble, Borders, etc.